The Ultimate Monologue Book for Middle School Actors Volume I

111 One-Minute Monologues

A Smith and Kraus Book
Published by Smith and Kraus, Inc.
177 Lyme Road, Hanover, NH 03755
www.smithkraus.com

First Edition: October 2003
Manufactured in the United States of America
10 9 8 7 6 5 4 3 2 1

Cover and text design by Julia Gignoux, Freedom Hill Design

Library of Congress Cataloging-in-Publication Data
Dabrowski, Kristen.
111 one-minute monologues / Kristen Dabrowski.-- lst ed.
p. cm. -- (The ultimate audition book for middle school actors ;
1) (Young actors series)
Summary: A collection of 111 original monologues, each about one
minute long, to be used by male or female middle school actors for
auditions and other purposes.
ISBN 1-57525-346-1
1. Monologues--Juvenile literature. 2. Acting--Juvenile literature.
[1. Monologues. 2. Acting.] I. Title: One hundred and eleven one-minute
monologues. II. Title. III. Series. IV. Young actor series
PN2080 .D33 2003
812'.6--dc22
2003057251

The Ultimate Monologue Book for Middle School Actors VOLUME I

• • •

111 One-Minute Monologues

Kristen Dabrowski

YOUNG ACTORS SERIES

A Smith and Kraus Book

THE ULTIMATE AUDITION BOOK FOR TEENS SERIES

The Ultimate Audition Book for Teens Volume 1:
111 One-Minute Monologues by Janet Milstein

The Ultimate Audition Book for Teens Volume 2:
111 One-Minute Monologues by L. E. McCullough

The Ultimate Audition Book for Teens Volume 3:
111 One-Minute Monologues by Kristen Dabrowski

The Ultimate Audition Book for Teens Volume 4:
111 One-Minute Monologues by Debbie Lamedman

The Ultimate Audition Book for Teens Volume 5:
111 Shakespeare Monologues

THE ULTIMATE SCENE STUDY SERIES FOR TEENS

The Ultimate Scene Study Series for Teens Volume 1:
60 Shakespeare Scenes

The Ultimate Scene Study Series for Teens Volume 2:
60 Short Scenes by Debbie Lamedman

To Walter, Louise, Danielle, Joel, and Adrienne
for their love and support.

To Rebecca for making me do this.

CONTENTS

Introduction

Hello, actors! As a professional actor for eleven years now, I know how hard the search for the perfect monologue can be. A monologue should be immediate, active, and fun. You shouldn't mind having to say it over and over when you're practicing, auditioning, or performing it. You should be able to relate to it. This is difficult when you're in middle school. Most plays are written for adults. Then where are you supposed to get monologues from? This book. Here are some tips on approaching monologues:

- Pick the monologue that hits you. Trust your instincts. You'll pick the right one!

- Make the monologues active. What do you want and how do you try to get it? Pressure? Flattery? Characters often try lots of different approaches to get their way.

- Who are you talking to and where are they? Some monologues have you speaking to more than one person. Make sure you make this as clear as possible.

- Do you get answered or interrupted? Be sure to fill in words in your head for the moments when you are spoken to in the monologue, even if it's a simple yes or no.

- How do you feel about the person or people you are talking to? For example, you speak a lot differently to your best friend than you do to your math teacher.

- Notes about stage directions and terminology: The word *beat* or the start of a new paragraph indicates another character speaks or a new idea arises. *Pause* or other stage directions like *shocked* are suggestions, but do not need to be observed absolutely. *Seriocomic* means the monologue can be both serious and/or comic. You'll figure it out for yourself — see what comes up!

- Keep it real. Bring these characters to life as only you can.

Final notes: These monologues stand alone as solo pieces (and are not from full-length plays). However, if you want to put together a showcase of monologues, you'll see that some pieces work very well together because they are a continuation of a story line or because they discuss the same subject. Feel free to mix and match. Enjoy!

Kristen Dabrowski

Female Monologues

SECRETS AND LIES

Kyra, dramatic

Where's my diary? Griffiiiiiiiiin! Where are you? Do you have my diary? You better not or I'll chop your little head off! Where are you hiding?

I'm going in your room! I'm going to look in your underwear drawer!

A-ha! There you are. OK, little schmuck, where's my diary? You don't know? I don't believe you. I have not forgotten that you stole my school uniform and cut little holes in it last year. Everyone saw my underwear! So from now until the rest of the eternity, I will not trust you. Anything that goes missing, anything out of place, anything at all, and I am coming right for you, little brother.

Now where's my diary? Fess up now and maybe I'll only torture you for a few days —

Mom? What's that in your hand? That's — my diary! You didn't!

My life is a nightmare! I can't trust anyone!

TWO CUPS OF HUMILIATION

Monica, seriocomic

Please don't talk to the lady, Mom. We can do this without her.
I don't know which one I like. I don't care. Anything. Let's just
get something, if we must, and get out of here!

No, no. I don't want to be measured. It's not necessary. Let's
just grab one and get out.

You're kidding, right? That's an old-lady bra, Mom. That's,
like, for an eighty year old. No, I *don't* care; it just can't be an
old-lady one.

No. You can't come in the dressing room and neither can
the sales lady. Geez, do you act like this with Susie? Or
Grandma? Honestly, Mom, don't get all excited about this. It's
just a stupid bra.

NEVER-NEVER LAND

Penny, seriocomic

What's the big deal about growing up? My sister says everyone is mean in seventh grade. And they don't have a playground even. And she looks in her mirror every day, facing sideways, to see if she's any bigger. Like this. *(Pulling her shirt tight across her chest, sucking in her cheeks, and looking at herself from the side, face out front.)* She looks stupid. Like a fish.

I'm always going to be a kid. I mean it. Who says you can't? I'll maybe get older but I'll still have fun.

When you grow up, you can't dance to the oldies in the kitchen in your socks or draw with those smelly markers. No, you can't. You can't. I swear it. OK, if you're an artist you can draw, but that's it. You have to go to parties and kiss. You have to study. You have to drink coffee. You have to sit up straight. You have to wear eye makeup that runs down your face and makes you look eighty and tired. Everyone tries to be the same, all laughing the same and walking the same and talking the same. My sister and her friends talk on and on and on and think they are so funny, but they're not. They never go outside. They go to the mall and they don't even buy anything. They just stand around.

No way. Not gonna do it. And no one can make me. Not you, not anyone.

LITERATURE LOSERS

Avril, seriocomic

Why does everyone think this story is so sad? I think Romeo and Juliet were stupid. Can you imagine — actually stabbing yourself in the chest? Pushing the knife in. You'd probably have to bleed to death. It would take ages. No boy is worth that. No way.

And being married when you're fourteen? Gross. Completely gross. The whole thing is wrong. And I think that friar who marries them and tries to help them out should be arrested. And the nurse who thinks it's all so cute? What a wacko!

I don't know why these two families are fighting in the first place anyhow. Can't we all just get along?

Tell you what, if my parents found out I married some dork when I was fourteen, they'd kill me before I had a chance to do it myself. I'd be so dead. I wouldn't be allowed to leave my room 'til I was forty!

THE ART OF ME

Yvonne, seriocomic

(Looking at a picture in a magazine.)
Bleh. She's ugly. I think.

I saw in a book the most amazing, beautiful thing. It's on the wall in my room. I had my dad blow up the picture on the computer and he can print it out really big at work. It's this statue. *(Beat.)* Don't make fun; it's for real. You should see it. It's a woman. It used to be on the front of a ship, but it fell off. It's really big. White. She's sort of whitish gray. Her hair? She doesn't have a head. *(Beat.)* No, don't laugh!

Listen. I'll tell you what's so beautiful about that. She is strong. Not like Arnold Schwartzenegger. Like no one I've ever seen. Like Mia Hamm, sort of. The soccer player. She's sort of elegant and strong and wearing this long dress — You can see her legs. And it's a sort of light dress with wind blowing it around, like it would have been on the front of the boat. And she has wings! Wouldn't you love to have wings?

So, anyway, I want to look like her. I don't want to look like that skinny monster in the magazine. I want to look like I could be on the front of a huge ship. Like that dumb scene in *Titanic.* Only different. Promise me you won't hate me when I'm soooo beautiful.

GROWTH SPURT

Sophie, seriocomic

Mom, Yvonne has gone mad. Bonkers. Loopy. She wants to be a character in a movie or a piece of art. I just want to be a sixth grader people like. Why is it so hard? *(Beat.)* I don't want to talk about it.

But — Mom — they took that sweater you bought me for my birthday. I don't know why. *(Beat.)* NO! You can't tell anyone. I just wish I could have it back. And I don't know why they pick on me. And I know you bought it for me so, I'm sorry.

I know it's not my fault, but — maybe it is. Maybe if I knew what to say and do they wouldn't have done it. And I've tried to be nice and to — see how they act so maybe they would — But it doesn't work. It only makes it worse.

And, and . . . I think it's kind of your fault. Because you made me a little girl and I can't say anything bad and I can't stay up late and watch "Sex in the City." Yes, they do watch it. Their parents let them. I need to be more adult, Mom. I need to say words you don't like. *(Beat.)* Yes, yes, I do. *(Beat.)* I'm not better than them, Mom. I'm not. I'm worse. I don't have friends. *(Beat.)* OK, I have Yvonne, but did you forget already, Mom? She's nuts!

BEST FRIENDS

Lindsey, dramatic

Are you mad at me? *(Beat.)* You never talk to me anymore. We were best friends.

Remember when we had a picnic in the mall? 'Cause it rained? And we went to the movies? We saw that movie with George Clooney, which we didn't get, but we thought he was cute? *(Pause.)* Why won't you talk to me anymore? *(Beat.)* Why do I bother you? I didn't DO anything. Can't you be friends with Laurie and Jackie and be friends with me, too? You don't have to JUST hang around with them. *(Beat.)* Well, I don't like them either, so what?

They make fun of you. You do anything they want you to and they laugh at you. You're not one of them. *(Beat.)* I know I'm not one of them either. But I don't care. I just do what we like to do — walk in the stream, catch lightning bugs, have sleepovers —

It's not baby stuff. You used to like it. You still do. Sure, you laugh all the time, but you're not really laughing. You're pretending, I can tell. *(Beat.)* Well, I don't care if I'm a baby. Fine. I'll be a baby, but I'll laugh for real. And no one will be laughing at me.

I don't want to be your friend anymore. You're mean now.

NORMAL

Nadia, seriocomic

Ugh. This bagel has a long, black *hair* in it. I'm starving, too. I must have the worst karma in the world.

See, everyone thinks my life is so different, so glamorous, but I get hairs in my bagel. I'm just a normal girl!

Who am I kidding? You are the only friend I still have. They tell me to tell everyone in interviews that I'm "normal" 'cause I go to regular school. People look at me like I've got four heads now — each with six eyes, three noses, and no teeth! Just 'cause I'm on TV.

Be my best friend and get me a new bagel? PLEASE. I'll love you forever. I'll be your best friend forever — please, please, please? You are THE BEST. Really. I'm going to tell people from now on "I'm not normal, but my best friend is." That's a big compliment in my book.

AND THE WINNER IS . . .

Tyra, seriocomic

I'd like to thank the Academy, my agent, and, of course, my friends and family who supported me along the way to my success. To Mr. Greene, Sara Simonsen, Mrs. Moupe, Rich Glick, and Lynn Dixie, I'd like to say on national TV that you didn't contribute to this award at all. In fact, you stink. You stink like bad cheese. You were mean and nasty and unfair.

To all the cast and crew, thank you. You made me what I am today: a successful, award-winning, beloved actress. Lastly, I'd like to say to all the kids who have dreams of doing this, keep dreaming. Hold onto those dreams. And don't worry if you don't get the lead in the school play. I didn't. And look at me now. Only kids who kiss the teachers' butts get the leads. Be yourself. And the Mrs. Moupes of the world won't matter at all when you're a big star.

Thank you, America! I love you!

THIS LAND IS MY LAND

Meg, comic

Yeah. I discovered this country. It's mine. That's my flag over there. With the brightly colored flowers. Kind of Hawaiian but with a sophisticated flair. I'm going to call this place Megania. Or Meganland. United States of Megan. I got it — Mega Mega. Like it? I do.

I've always been an explorer, really. Interested in discovering new things. One day, I just started walking and never stopped. I walked across hills, I walked across dales, I swam oceans. Frankly, it was tiring. But it's all worth it now. My very own land.

I plan to be Empress. No, Queen. No, Ruler of All She Surveys. I'll have a tiara. And you won't. Yes, my name is spelled M-E-G-A-N. Get it right in the papers.

What's next? I'm torn between discovering a mountain or an ocean or an island or a planet. Or maybe I'll just stay here and live the good life. Don't just stand there. Start making me a throne! I told you, I'm tired.

You're going to have to start anticipating my whims, people.

STAR SPANGLED BUNGLER

Faith, seriocomic

(Singing "Star Spangled Banner.")
   Oh say can you —
   Oh say can you —
   Rocket's —
   I'm — I'm sorry. I can't remember — ANYTHING!
   I need to breathe deeply. And relax. Sorry. I'm OK
now. Yes.
   Oh say can you SEE
   By the dawn's early —
   This has never happened to me before. Never! I'm a pro-
fessional. And I must have sung this song and *heard* this song
ten billion times! I can do this. I was fine in rehearsal. So, here
we go.
   Oh say — There are a lot of you. A lot. Why are you all
staring at me? Stop it! Go away! Just —
   I have to go home now. Daddy? Where's the car? Let's make
a run for it!

PLAY TIME

Renée, comic

OK, let's play. I'm the teacher; you're the student.

Now, Jimmy, you've been very bad. *(Beat.)* No, you cannot go to the bathroom before we start. The bell has rung. Sit in your seat! What is six times 4,832? You don't know? Go sit in the corner, next to Susie. I don't care if you hate Susie! Don't look at me, look at the wall. No talking!

I'll tell you what. If you can answer one question, I'll let you join the rest of the class again. And we were just about to fingerpaint. Don't move. I said you have to answer one question, *correctly*, to join us. OK, Jimmy.

If a train is traveling out of a station in Dallas, Texas, at three o'clock at nine miles per hour and another train is traveling out of Austin, Texas at three miles per hour, how much does a soda cost at the train's snack bar?

Wrong! Now face the corner again.

No, you cannot be the teacher now. You can't even finish kindergarten.

TABLE FOR TWO

Phoebe, seriocomic

See that? Those two on a date? *(Beat.)* Yeah, that's not the weird part. The weird part is how they're sitting. Right next to each other. I don't get that. Wouldn't you normally sit across from the person you're with when there's only two of you? When you sit like that, one right next to the other, you can't talk. You'd get a crick in your neck from holding your head to one side all night.

And if they're sitting like that to kiss — well, it's a restaurant for goodness sake. People are eating here. I don't want to look at that. Two dopes staring all googily-eyed at each other and slobbering all over. Give me a break. And think about it — you eat and little bits of food get caught in your teeth, right? So, if you kiss someone — Ugh! I can't even think about it. It's just too uggy.

It looks like they're riding the bus. Weird.

LIKE LIKE

Michelle, seriocomic

Stephen likes me? Oh. OK.

I don't know what to tell you to tell him. I don't know what to think! I mean, I guess that's nice. It *is* nice. Tell him thanks. Is that leading him on? I don't want to lead him on. I don't know. About all this. You know, this "liking" stuff.

Do I like someone else? Well, no. But don't tell him that. Because I don't think I *like* him like him. Know what I mean? I just like him. But don't tell him that either. That wouldn't be nice.

Aaah! I don't know! Tell him; tell him —

Tell him you didn't tell me! Tell him I didn't hear you because a big truck drove by!

I need time. This is all happening too fast!

POT PARTY

Bridget, seriocomic

Pot. That's what she's into now. Pot. She asked me to go to her party and that we could smoke it and it would be fun and I should try it. *(Beat.)* I know I can't go! If I did, I wouldn't tell *you.* Oops! I don't even think I want to, actually. Is that abnormal? It is, I think. Should I want to? I'm supposed to be in my rebellious stage.

What do you mean *we* can have a pot party? Pots and pans. Hahahaha. You're a laugh riot, Mom. I can't believe you even said that. *(Beat.)* OK, so it made me laugh. Because it's *so* dumb! You're nuts, you know that?

Listen, I'm going to go to my room and mope and play music you hate way too loud so I don't feel like I'm [twelve] going on one hundred. I might even call my friends and talk about how horrible you are. It's nothing personal.

ONE BIG CHANCE

Ruby, seriocomic

Dad, don't stand too close. You'll embarrass me. *(Beat.)* My shirt is OK. This is how people dress now. Look around. *(Beat.)* No! Please, don't look at me when you're talking.

Well, of course everyone knows I have parents. Everyone has parents. But not everyone's parents come stand in line with them.

Dad, this is so important to me. I have to get this. *(Beat.)* I know, I know, I can't get my hopes up. But this is my dream and you can't have dreams without hoping a little, right? Don't touch my hair. It is integral to my "look," carefully constructed from viewing numerous pictures of Whitney, Mariah, and Britney, not to mention last year's winner of the contest.

I am so nervous! What if they make fun of me, Dad? What if I'm a joke? *(Beat.)* I know. I don't have to do this. But I have to.

I'm next. It's OK! I'm calm. *(Beat.)* No! I can't drink that. Soda is bad for you vocal chords. But — thanks, Daddy. How about you buy me ice cream later?

KEEP OUT

Ashley, comic

Mom! That is *my* skirt! What are you doing in my room? In my *closet*? That is private, Mom. What do you want with my stuff anyway? It's *mine*. *(Beat.)* So you bought it, but you bought it for *me* so it's *mine*. Not yours.

You're — you're old, Mom. You shouldn't be wearing my stuff. It makes you look — old! *(Beat.)* I'm not jealous; I'm realistic. You're supposed to look like a mom, not like a high school student. You are one step away from being on Jerry Springer. All you have to do is seduce one of my friends — You wouldn't do that would you, Mom???! *(Beat.)* It's not a crazy thing to say. I'm serious. Borrowing my clothes is the first step.

Don't do it, Mom. Don't do it. Put the skirt down and step away from the closet. I don't want you to be on Springer or go to prison for seducing teenagers. Please, I'm begging you; go buy a sweater set. Please, Mom. Let's drive to Talbots *now*.

TOO MUCH

Sara, dramatic

Did you ever want to kill yourself? Don't tell anyone, but I did. It's kind of embarrassing. Well — promise you won't laugh — I went downstairs to the kitchen and ate *all* of the Flintstone vitamins. I didn't eat the orange ones because I don't like how they taste — like baby aspirin. *(Beat.)* Duh, I should not have taken baby aspirin because — hello? — I don't like how it tastes! My mom *really* yelled at me and said I was stupid. I couldn't believe she said that. That night I wrote on her mirror "I HATE YOU" with her best red lipstick, because I did hate her, and she woke me up at three AM to make me clean it off. She doesn't understand me at all! I want her to feel bad inside, the way I do. I want her to notice — it sounds so stupid when you say it out loud. She thinks I'm melodramatic, that's what she calls me, but I'm just being REAL. I'm just being ME. She just doesn't understand me.

DIRT — NOT THE GOOD KIND

Christina, comic

This is overrated. Vacation. Camping. Don't get me wrong, I'm glad not to be in school but — sleeping outside? Isn't that why houses were invented? The ground is always lumpy. And eating outside is so annoying. I swear I've eaten one hundred bugs. I can't even think about it. Remember yesterday there was a bee in my soda can and it went in my mouth and I spit it out and it was still alive and flew away?

Even birds build nests. They don't want to sleep on the ground either. Plus, it's cold. Why can't we just have one of those Disney World vacations? You know, go on rides, stay in a *hotel*, see some dolphins jump around or something?

Yeah. Dolphins and hotels with cable TV. That's the life. Just an idea for next year, Dad.

NOT SO SLIM GYM

Carrie, comic

No. *(Beat.)* That's exactly what I mean — No! Why? Why should I? Nothing's chasing me. What's the point of running if nothing's chasing you? *(Beat.)* You don't count, Miss Roper. *(Beat.)* Because you don't scare me.

You have a point there. I probably will be out of shape and not be able to run if wild animals are chasing me. But then again, don't underestimate adrenaline. It's a powerful thing. I think it could pull me through if, say, a tiger gets set loose on the track.

Look, maybe we can compromise. What if I run in slo-mo and sing the theme from *Rocky*? *(Beat.)* No? *Chariots of Fire*? *(Beat.)* *The Bionic Woman*? *(Beat.)* You're right; I don't even know that one. What if I tell you I have cramps? *(Beat.)* OK. I'll be sitting over here on the bench if you need me.

BARF AND BAGGY SHORTS

Rebecca, seriocomic

Yuck. Gross. Totally disgusting. I think I'm going to cry. This is not fair. *He* gets sick and I have to clean up after him. Why couldn't he get sick on his own math book? It's on my book and my clothes! I'm going to smell like this all day! Do you think I can go home? *(Beat.)* Can I just throw my book away? *(Beat.)* It's got his lunch all over it! This is *so* unfair! I am being punished for what he did wrong! *(Beat.)* OK, maybe he couldn't help it, but . . .

I should get *his* math book and he should get mine. That's the only fair thing. I shouldn't have to deal with this for the whole rest of the year.

I can't believe this. I have to wear my gym clothes all day. This couldn't be more humiliating.

ST. VINCENT BLUES

Mimi, comic

Gee, green socks or navy-blue socks? Having a uniform is so *great*. They look so *cool* and I get to pick out the color of my sweater *and* the color of my socks. I am one lucky, lucky girl. Who wants to wear jeans and T-shirts when they could wear *this* lovely ensemble? I tell you?

The only saving grace is that we can roll our skirts up. That makes it almost cute. Doesn't it? Who am I kidding? It's *hopeless!* We can't go to the mall like this. The public school kids will kill us!

We have no choice. We have to run in packs. Like wolves. Safety in numbers. We have to get Gina and Bridget to come, too.

I wish I'd worn the blue socks!

TROUBLE WITH TP

Elyse, comic

(Back to the audience.) Toilet paper is good for lots of things.
(Turning around. Shirt is stuffed with lots of toilet paper.)
And, if you wet it just enough, it sticks to the ceiling for all time and no one will *ever* be able to get it off!

(Pretending to throw gobs of wet toilet paper on the ceiling.) Hey, Mrs. Stinktrousers —

THIS is for giving me detention for talking too much in class!

THIS is for yelling at me for passing a note in science class!

THIS is for separating me from my best friend, Jennie, because we were LAUGHING while you were talking!

THIS is for —

What? *(Looking behind.)* Uh-oh.

BODYGUARD

Paris, seriocomic

Why don't you pick on someone your own size? Huh? What did he ever do to you, you little stinky brat? Why don't you just take a seat and shut your big mouth?

He doesn't need me to fight for him. He can fight for himself. But you made me mad, and if you want to beat up on someone, you can start with *me*. Someone your own size, you caveman.

Come on. Bring it on. I dare you.

Why are you just sitting there? Scared, baby?

Listen; if you *ever* touch my brother again, you are dead meat. I mean it. You may be big for a fourth grader, but I'm going to be bigger than you for a lot of years. You'd better start being nice, you little maggot.

BEAUTY IS PAIN, PAIN IS PAINFUL

Mia, comic

I've wanted to do this for a long time. I've wanted to do this for a long time. I've wanted —

I'm just reminding myself of why I'm sitting in this chair. Because I've wanted to do this for a long time. I'm not going to turn back now. After all, here I am. I'm even in the chair. Waiting. This is taking a long time.

What's that?? *(Beat.)* Oh, ice. To numb them. So I won't feel it. The needle. Going into my earlobes. Has anyone ever been stabbed in the neck by the piercing gun-thing? *(Beat.)* You know, have you ever missed or has it ever gone through their ears and into their neck? *(Beat.)* Has anyone ever bled to death or gotten a horrible infection? *(Beat.)* Everything's sterile, right?

This is going to hurt a lot, isn't it? Maybe this isn't a good idea. I wanted to have pierced ears, I wanted to buy cute earrings, lots of other girls in my class have pierced ears, but —

OUCH! Oh, is that it? That wasn't too bad. OK. Let's do the other ear. Is that . . . blood? *(Beat.)* Maybe I'll just go with the one. Call it a day. The pirate look. Go home to my mommy. I don't need both —

OUCH!

Thank you.

THE PLAN

Samantha, comic

Open the door. *My* door, Sam. I want to be treated with respect, like a princess. *(Beat.)* Thank you for driving us, Mr. Zimmerman!

What will we be doing this evening? *(Beat.)* Dinner — good; movie — good; and . . . and what? What are you insinuating? *(Beat.)* I'm not *accusing* you of anything. I just feel you should know that you cannot *expect* anything from me.

To lighten things a bit, let me tell you the upside of all this. If you play your cards right, here's what you have to look forward to. After we've been together for a week, we'll kiss, moving to French kissing after two weeks. We will get that to a science over the next several months. This is a skill that will help you throughout life. As for the rest, the other "bases," they will come slowly as our love grows. And I will not get married until at *least* two years after college because I will not be one of those sad women getting an M.R.S. in college. But there's really no need to worry because I think I want babies with black hair and your hair is light brownish.

Now let's go have a really good time!

EVOLUTION

Belle, comic

That's it. I'm giving up men for good. I've had enough. The waiting. The lipstick. The disappointment. Pretending you like things
you don't like and laughing at jokes that aren't funny. Worry-
ing you're sweating too much or breathing too much or gig-
gling too much or not enough. Eating *salad* instead of spaghetti
— I'm done. That's it. Don't even try to change my mind. I'm
very stubborn when I've set my mind to something.

    I don't need to get married. I don't need babies. I am a care-
free, independent WOMAN. Who wants to get tied down? If
I did, then I couldn't travel to Egypt to see the Pyramids or Italy
to see the Sistine Chapel — there's just too much to do and too
little time. I don't feel like compromising. Know what? I'm going
to be the smartest person in school. I'm going to speak out for
what I believe in. Oh, yes, those morons will beg me to go out
with them — someday, after puberty maybe, when I'm a famous
writer and they've evolved a little — but I will refuse them.

    "NO!" Just practicing.

BATTLE OF THE BAND (MEMBERS)

Veronica, comic

He's mine. You can't like him! I like him *more*. You have to like someone else in the band. We can't both like the same person. *(Beat.)* Why? It's just the rules; that's why. We're friends and we can't like the same guy in the band and I called John. So you have to pick someone else. May I suggest Tony? He's not as gross as Rich and dances better than Tommy.

Mary! I don't know if we can be friends now. And you've been my best friend for this whole year! I've liked John since before you even knew the band existed. I had their CD first. I have seen every one of their videos, and I begged and begged and begged until my parents let me stay up to see the making of the video special.

OK, you're going to make fun of me, but here's the deal. I want to marry him. I'm going to go to a concert, and he's going to see me and then we're going to go out, and we're going to live happily ever after. I really think so. You can't marry him because he's already going to be married to me!

He'd never divorce me for you! That's it. Jackie is my best friend now because she likes Tommy. Maybe John and I will have you over to our beach house for dinner one day. Maybe.

CHEERLEAD

Brittany, comic

OK. You stand there. And Jenny, you're in the back. Don't argue, just do it. *(Beat.)* Because I'm the captain, that's why I can tell you what to do. It's my *job*. And not a very easy one, either. Now, are you going to get in the back or not? *(Beat.)* I am not bossy. I can't help it if I am the leader of this team. *You* voted me in. *(Beat.)* I am not different! Listen, if I don't take charge nothing will get done around here. Anyway, no one else thinks I'm bossy.

What? Amanda! *You* think I'm bossy? I can't believe that. Please. I have not been "corrupted by power." Give me a break. Look, are we going to stand here talking or are we going to get on with practice? I made up a whole new routine and it's really fresh — Of *course* I made up the new routine. What is the problem? I'm good at making them up; that's why I'm the *captain*. Now let's do it.

Jenny, you're in *back*. *(Beat.)* Where am I? In front, if you must know. Now shut your trap and listen up. *(In cheerleader voice.)* Let's go, Hornets!

JANUARY FIRST

Gwen, comic

I'm turning a new leaf this year. My New Year's resolution is to do *everything* differently. I am going to study. I am going to do all my homework all the time. I am going to get along with others. I am going to shave my legs on gym days. I am not going to mouth off. I am going to go on a diet. I am going to wear makeup, even when I don't want to. I'll iron my clothes. I'm going to mind my manners and respect my elders. I am going to do kind acts for less fortunate people. I'm going to help my parents around the house. I will go to church and not laugh or yawn. I am not going to complain when I have to visit my grandparents. I am going to join clubs and extracurricular activities. I promise I won't sit around dreaming about Doug Price who doesn't even know I'm alive. I am going to stop starting every sentence with "I."

I am destined to fail. I will start tomorrow.

WELCOME TO THE
TWENTY-FIRST CENTURY

Trina, seriocomic

What year is it? No, really, what year is it? *(Beat.)* I'm not saying it because *I* don't know; I'm saying it because *you* don't
know. You really don't. It's 2004 and you are actually telling
me I can't wear makeup.

Don't walk away. This is a serious discussion. Maybe you
know the year intellectually, but you don't understand what it
means to live in 2004. It is the new millennium, Dad. Girls wear
makeup. Girls who are way younger than me wear makeup. It
does not make you a hooker or anything. Everyone does it. I
know *you* don't care what other people do, but *I* care what other
people do.

I *would* jump off a bridge if *every* other person in my grade
did. What's wrong with that? How can you think putting on
makeup is the same thing as jumping off a bridge anyhow? That
is sick, Dad. I mean it. Last time I checked, putting on makeup
did not make you *die*.

What wearing makeup does mean is that I can have friends,
that I can go places with my friends, that I can look better, that
I can go on dates — don't freak out! OK, OK. One thing at a
time. Sooooo, can I have this lip gloss already or what?

CREATIVE CONCEALER

Anastasia, comic

(Standing with her hand on her cheek, trying to look normal.)
Ohmygod, Jeannie! I'm so glad to see you! I need help, ASAP!
Look!
(Moves hand from cheek for a nanosecond.) You didn't see?
I can't believe it, it's so big — how could you not see it! It's —
a zit. A Z-I-T. The size of Kansas.

I cannot go through this entire day like *this*! Believe it or
not, it's hard to make this *(Points to the hand already on face.)*
look casual. Do you have any makeup? *(Beat.)* Lip gloss?! What
am I going to do with lip gloss?

Ohmygod! You're a genius! IloveyouIloveyouIloveyou!
(Pushes her hair over her face.) How do I look? Excellent!

THAT'S SO WRONG

Lyric, comic

Javier, we don't do that here. *(Beat.)* Well, you seem to be flirting with my mother. I know you're an exchange student and you're from another culture and all that, but it's a little weird. Really.

Don't say my mom is hot! She's my *mom*, Javier. *(Beat.)* Yes, she's attractive. Thank you. But she's not HOT. So, will you stop?

What do you mean? Are you telling me you flirt with my mom so she'll do your laundry? That's so unfair! Well, she doesn't do *my* laundry. I do it myself. She does *your* laundry?! She told me I had to learn to be an adult and take care of my own stuff. That's wrong. I'm going to yell at her. And I'm going to tell her what you said!

You think I'm pretty? Thanks, Javier. That's really nice. Hey! Stay where you are. Don't come any closer to me, lover boy. I'm onto you!

BLIND FOOL

Kirsty, comic

What?! You have to stop asking me what the board says. I can't read everything off to you. Listen, mister, I hate to break it to you, but you need glasses. You're blind! OK, not blind, but you have two choices:

Sit in front, like maybe a few inches from the board, OR *get glasses!*

Sorry, Mr. Sparr. Nothing's wrong.

See? You keep getting me in trouble. I'm not trying to be mean, but it's time to face facts. Besides, glasses are cute.

Not that I'm saying you're cute or anything. I mean, don't get any ideas here. I'm just thinking about, oh, Harry Potter, and, ah, other celebrities. *(Beat.)* I don't know who, just other people.

Hey, they are not nerdy! *I* wear glasses. And *I'm* cute. You'd know that if you weren't blind.

FAME

Alicia, comic

Ooo! I have the best idea. Why don't we jump up on the lunch tables and sing and dance like on TV? *(Beat.)* I don't know what we'd sing. Maybe a song from chorus! Like "Jingle Bell Rock"! *(Beat.)* Why not? Maybe everyone will join in with us! *(Beat.)* OK, maybe not everyone. *(Beat.)* How should I know what dance steps we'd do? Maybe everyone wouldn't be doing the same steps — no! Wait! We could do the hokey pokey! Everyone knows that! I'll do it if you do it. Come on, pleeeeeeeease? Pleeeeeeeeeeeeeease???? It'll be fun!

Ready? On the count of three. One, two, three —

Ha, ha, ha! No *way* I'd do that! I can't believe you fell for it! You look so stupid! Everyone was staring, too! I give you points for having guts, though!

Hey, where are you going? It was funny! Wait up!

FREAKING OUT

Charlie, seriocomic

What are we doing at your party on Friday night? *(Beat.)* Really? Yeah, that will be fun. I guess. Couldn't we watch a comedy? Like *Ace Ventura*? My mom never wants me to watch that. She says it's crude. We could watch that. *(Beat.)* I'm not crazy about scary movies. I don't understand why people like to be scared — I hate it!

When I was in third grade, in art class, Ellen told me about the movie *The Exorcist* where this girl our age gets possessed by the devil. *(Beat.)* No! Don't make me see it.

What I was going to say is that ever since I *heard* about that movie I stay awake at night, and I think I will be possessed or that my little sister who shares a room with me (which I hate) will be possessed. And I can't decide which is worse. Being possessed myself or being stuck in the room with a possessed person. I stare at her face in the dark to see if it starts changing. She grinds her teeth when she sleeps so sometimes I think it's happening; she's getting possessed.

The only way not to get possessed is to be really religious. I hate church so I'm a goner. At the same time, the devil likes to take over girls the most because they aren't as bad as adults. I just can't win! Can we *please, please* see *Ace Ventura* on Friday?

PARTY TIME

Jessica, comic

I've got it all planned out.

At six, we eat hamburgers and fries.

At six-thirty we eat cake. Oh, and everyone sings "Happy Birthday," of course.

At seven, we watch a scary horror movie and scream our heads off and practically wet ourselves because we won't walk to the bathroom by ourselves because we're afraid of the dark.

I'm guessing somewhere in there my stupid brother tries to scare us. Oh, and we eat popcorn during the movie and cheese curls.

Then we put in my sister's makeup at nine and paint our fingernails and toes at nine-thirty.

What else? We eat ice cream. We tell ghost stories. I know this one about a man who gets killed — I'll tell it later.

No sleeping allowed. Oh, and someone barfs. Someone always barfs. I dunno why.

DON'T EVEN

Kate, comic

What was that? Hello? Anyone there? Listen; if you think you're funny you're mistaken. I've got a really big dog here who's very hungry so I wouldn't suggest coming in. And there are lots of adults here now. You might *think* I'm baby-sitting, but I'm not!

Don't even try to kill me. My dad, the chief of police and a former assassin for the U.S. Government is in the next room! He's just taking a little nap. I'm going to wake him up now . . .

Listen, I'm not even scared of you, so terrorizing me will bring you no pleasure. I'm not even going to run. I'm just going to sit here, watching TV. And don't even try to call; I've seen that movie and I know your game. If I don't answer the phone, you can't breathe heavily into it, and I can't trace the call and find out the call is coming from IN THE HOUSE, so don't bother. It's impossible to freak me out. If you want to tear out my guts, just politely say so and we'll discuss options. OK?

Hello?

WOO-HOO

Lori, comic

Is it me or has the "woo-hoo" gotten WAY out of hand? Couldn't we make another sound like "uh-huhhhh" or "hail, Caesar"! What if we just clapped politely? It just drives me up a wall.

My EX-friend, Cathy, used to say woo-hoo all the time. No homework in English class: Woo-hoo! Let's go have pizza: Woo-hoo! There's an ant on your foot: Woo-hoo! Everything got a big woo-hoo. It's stupid and annoying. Just like Cathy.

I bet she let out the biggest woo-hoo of her life when she got a date with my ex-boyfriend. I knew she liked him all along, but I never thought she'd stoop so low. Can you believe I caught her sitting on his lap in the lunchroom last week? Seconds after he told me he didn't want to see me anymore. Coincidence? I don't think so. Tramp. They deserve each other. He actually said, "It's not you, it's me. I need to work some stuff out." Oh, is that what they're calling it these days? Working stuff out? She didn't say anything at all. I had to find out the hard way — seeing them together.

I can't wait until he dumps *her*. Know what I'll say? Uh-huhhhhhhhh!

WHAT A GIRL REALLY WANTS

Helen of Troy, seriocomic

You think this is great? Romantic? Exciting? Live my life, sister. This is terrible. Two boys fighting over me. Do they ask me what I think? No, of course not. I'm not sure I like either of them. I'm not sure either of them like me. They don't even know me. They just say I'm pretty. "Oh, Helen, you're so pretty." "Helen, your lips are like rosebuds." Rosebuds. They really do say that. See what I'm saying? It's a little icky. Plus, half the time they show up to see me with black eyes and split lips from fighting each other. Ugh! Maybe they are cute, but how would I know? I only see them when they're a wreck, all black and blue. I think they think it impresses me.

I think I'd like one nice boy who doesn't get in fights and asks me what I *think* about things *and* listens to my answers!

THE OTHER BOY GEORGE

Martha Washington, comic

He has wooden teeth? You can't make me marry him! He's a soldier. So, he's dirty. Mom! If I kiss him, I'll get splinters! It's wrong and you can't make me!

What's his name? *(Beat.)* George? That's a terrible name. George Washington. Ick. Sounds like he's a nerd. George Washington.

Dad, I don't care what you say; you can't make me marry some icky old smelly soldier who spends his life camping out in the dirt. Plus, isn't he a revolutionary? What if he's on the losing side? What then? I'll be an outcast! I'll be the wife of a traitor! No money, no friends — maybe I'd even go to jail!

Please don't make me do this. I can feel it in my bones. This George Washington is bad news.

YOU AIN'T MY PARTNER

Annie Oakley, comic

Get outta my way. I'll punch your lights out, mister. You better hightail it outta here; you're makin' me mad. *(Beat.)* I may be shorter than you, but I've got more gumption and a whole lot more smarts than a chump like you. Bring it on, bubba.

(Throwing one punch. Then talking to the ground.) I may be a lotta things, but I ain't a liar; I warned you.

(Looking eye level again.) Don't ever call me "missy" or "little girl" again. I'm grown up if you haven't noticed. I have *lived* life. I have *seen* the world. I have survivor skills. So don't be telling me I'm too little or too young to do anything. I can do anything and everything I wanna do. That includes flattening you like a weasel under a wagon wheel. And don'cha forget it, mister!

SWEET

Dairy Queen, comic

Go on. Have ice cream for dinner. And breakfast. And lunch! You know you want to. All the cool kids are doing it. Come on. No one's here but you and me. Who will know?

Who am I? The Dairy Queen, of course! Don't forget chocolate sauce. And whipped cream. Mmm-mmmm!

I am not gaining a few pounds! Besides, a little cushioning is healthy. Otherwise, it hurts to sit down. Have some crushed up Oreos on that.

Plus, this outfit isn't so flattering, so it's not fair to judge my appearance. I have to dress like a German five-year-old. I can't believe anyone chooses to wear clogs. They're uncomfortable. Cherries. You need cherries. Food and people can never be too sweet!

You're a cutie. Wanna go out sometime for a hot fudge brownie sundae? With mint chocolate chip ice cream and caramel topping, of course.

E-GYPPED

Cleopatra, comic

Grapes — did that. Slaves fanning me with palm fronds — check. There's nothing to do. And it's so hot. A queen's life is so limited. I see all the same people; do all the same things. It's either grown-ups — boring advisors — or slaves. And I'm not supposed to talk to the servants. I listen in on their conversations, though. What's a "brat"? I bet they mean that I'm beautiful. That's what everyone tells me.

The Romans are coming again today. They are so loud. Everything's "ciao, bella" this and "ciao, bella" that. For them, being in Egypt is a vacation, a carnival cruise around the Nile. Wonder what Rome is like. They tell me it's beautiful with huge statues, blahblahblah. If it's so great, how come they come here? But I'll get to dress up, so who cares?

Bring me my big headdress, slave. No, not that one. The BIG one.

HAIR CARES

Karen, seriocomic

Why do they say blondes have more fun? I'm not having fun. If I have any fun it's because I planned everything and got everyone together and figured out what to do. Maybe the saying should be: "Being a blonde is hard work."

Also, the idea that this is the best time of my life is really stressing me out. If this is the best part, does that mean it's going to get worse?

Think about what we have to do every day. Go to school. Do homework. Deal with the jerks in our class. Try to fit in. Try to get good grades. Do chores at home. How am I supposed to have fun? What's fun about all that?

I can't wait until I'm eighty. My grandma gets to do whatever she wants. She goes to the movies. She eats cupcakes and candy all the time. She's got money to eat at the diner every day. *Grays* have more fun. I'm sure of it.

HALLOWEEN HORRORS

Jane, comic

Gray! It's gray. *Greenish* gray. It's awful! I can't go to school. I can't let anyone see me. I can't let my mom see me! She'll kill me. Oh no, I can't go to Rachel's party!

I don't understand. The black was supposed to wash out! It was supposed to wash out after five washings and I've washed it *ten* times! What am I gonna do? I hate Halloween. Can I dye it again without my hair falling out? Any other color — blonde, red, brown!

Don't just stand there; you have to help me! This is your fault. *(Beat.)* It is! You said you knew how to do this. You said it was easy. You *didn't* say, "Your hair will turn gray and you will have to live with hair the color of death for the rest of your life." I'm uglyyyyyyyyyyy. I look 486 years old! This is *wrong*!

Take me to a retirement home. I can't go back to school and I can't go home, so I may as well enjoy a few rounds of bingo before I die of embarrassment.

AWAY FROM HOME

Amanda, seriocomic

Have you ever boarded before? This is my first year.

On my questionnaire I said I liked soccer, reading, pop music, um . . . that I'm neat and fairly quiet.

Oh. *(Beat.)* No sports. *(Beat.)* No reading. Music? *(Beat.)* Rap, hip-hop. *(Beat.)* No, I don't like rap. Not even Eminem. I'm more of a Justin Timberlake person. I know it's cheesy, but, you know, I grew up with N*Sync and —

What? You don't believe in laundry? What do you mean? *(Beat.)* Never?? You *never* do laundry? Do you send it home? *(Beat.)* So, let's recap. You don't read, play sports, or do laundry. What do you do?

Oh. Oh. Ah, I'm not sure this is gonna work. I'm really quiet and —

Yeah. Let's go see someone about this *now*.

GO WEST, YOUNG WITCH

The Wicked Witch of the West, comic

It's not easy being green. Going to witch school puts me in such a bad mood. Everyone makes fun of me — the color of my skin, my wart, my laugh. My clothes aren't pretty and fashionable. They say only hicks come from out west.

I only have you, monkeys. You're my only friends.

You know, I *am* a witch. So how can they complain when I make their hair fall out after they call me names? I'm practicing. Doing my homework. They deserve it, those prissy witches from the east. I hate them.

I wish you could fly, monkeys, so we could get away from this place. Boarding school stinks. Why did my parents send my sister to a different school? Life is so bleak and dreary.

Monkeys, I'm going to find a way to make you fly. Would you like that? Would you be my best friends forever then?

Male Monologues

SCHOOL BOOKS, GHOUL BOOKS

Tom, comic

This book, *Pride and Prejudice,* is about . . . pride. And . . . prejudice. Prejudice is when you don't like people of other races. There's a girl named . . . Elizabeth and she's got lots of sisters. Um, and —

This book was boring and stupid. It was a book for girls. That part about her cousin wanting to marry her might make it sound sort of interesting, but it's not. I really would not recommend this book to anyone who was not a girl. I would, however, recommend Stephen King's book —

I'm sorry, Mrs. Shelby. It was boring. I couldn't do it. I tried. I really did. I did prepare another book report on Stephen King's *Cujo,* which is actually a very good book. It's long, too. Doesn't that count?

P.S. — Where does the prejudice come in? Isn't everyone white in England?

MAD DOG ON MAPLE

Shane, seriocomic

I'm not taking that way to school. No way. I made that mistake once. It's a shorter path, but there's a dog halfway down the block that's evil. I swear. It's black with red eyes and vicious pointy teeth. I had to run for blocks and blocks. I'm completely serious, man. This dog is insane. I bet his owner trained him to go after kids who walk past the house. Think about it. How come no one ever takes this shortcut? You've seen the news stories about kids being attacked by dogs. Seriously, I'm no chicken. And there's no way I'm letting that dog take a bite of me.

Let's take the long way around. It's worth it. Is it so bad if we're late? If you ask me, it's a good thing to miss five minutes of homeroom.

SUCKER

Ryan, comic

We're getting a dog? I'm allergic to dogs! You know that. I've always been allergic. My throat swells up and I can't breathe. My eyes itch like crazy —

(Beat.) What? You already did? He's here? His name is Mopey? You hate me, don't you? I can't believe Mom let you bring a dog into the house with my allergies. Where am I going to live now? I have to sleep in the garage!

MOM! We cannot get a dog! No, listen to me. You know I have serious allergies. Dust. Mold. Wheat. Eggs. Milk. And *dogs!* If I touch a dog, I will swell up. Now maybe you didn't consider this, but if there is a dog *in the house,* I will be around its hair or dander or whatever all the time! I will be sick all the time, Mom. So if we have a dog now, you are either going to have to get rid of it and all of our furniture and rugs or get rid of me. What's it going to be, Mom? The dog or me?

(Beat.) Oh, ha, ha, ha. You are so funny, dork. What a great joke. So funny I forgot to laugh. I hate you.

SPACE FACE

Jeff, comic

Yes, I'm completely ready for zero gravity. My mother always told me I didn't have my feet on the ground. So it'll be business as usual in space.

(Beat.) What else did my mother have to say to me? Well, she told me I'd better keep my room clean because all my stuff is going to be floating around the shuttle. *(Beat.)* Oh, nah, I didn't listen. I don't like being told what to do. I'll be able to see all the complicated equipment just fine, I'm sure.

I'm looking forward to eating the powderized, freeze-dried food. I've never eaten a hamburger out of a bag. I hope they put ketchup on it. I like a lot of ketchup.

Our mission is to break the sound barrier. With my experience playing my music too loud in my room, NASA thought I was the best man for the job. I was recommended highly by my neighbors for the job.

Well, I gotta take off now.

SUNDAY MORNING

Justin, comic

Ooooh. I'm so sick. I think I have a fever. And my armpits itch. Could I have the plague? Mom, I'm so sorry. I don't think I can go to church today.

Look out; I'm going to puke! Uhhhhh. I think I'm dying. Pray for me, Mom. When you're at church. Don't touch my forehead! I'm very sensitive. I could vomit on you. I'd better go back to bed. I'll just . . . oh, I don't know . . . maybe lie in bed . . . do some, uh, homework . . . maybe play a video game to, you know, pass the time. I'll be fine. Somehow. Go on, Mom. Go on without me.

(Beat.) Noooo! I really am! Really, really really! Have some pity. Awww, Mom. This stinks!

THE SLIME

Peter, comic

I have something to tell you. I wasn't paying attention in science class today. *(Beat.)* Don't yell at me! I'm not even finished telling you my story. So, I'm in science class and I thought the teacher said to mix together the two things on our desks. But we weren't supposed to do that. We were supposed to put them in different tubes with litmus paper or something.

So, anyway, I put them into the same tube. And, and —

(Beat.) OK! Brian Howell is green! I don't know how. I told you, I wasn't paying attention! But the goop overflowed from the tube and got on Brian and he's green. Just his hands, though. So he has to wear gloves, that's all.

(Beat.) I don't know if it will go away! I'm not a scientist! This is why I shouldn't have to take science. I'm a danger to myself and everyone around me!

THE PRINCIPAL'S SON

Ross, seriocomic

I know you're tired and you work all day. I know exactly what you mean, actually. I go to school all day, then I go to play football, then I have to do my homework. It's rough. Who even made up this stuff about us working five days a week and only getting two days off? That's insane. We have to take our lives back, Mom. We can't let The Man tell us what to do. *(Beat.)* I accept that people have to go to work and kids have to go to school. But what about going three days a week and having off four days a week? Think about it. Everyone would concentrate so much more. They'd be refreshed after such a long weekend. Heck, maybe you'd even be glad to be there. It's possible.

Don't laugh. Stress can kill people, Mom. You could have a heart attack, high blood pressure, all kinds of things. It's dangerous. Listen, you have a chance to make a difference here. You're the principal. You're in charge. And, as a nice little bonus, I'd be the most popular kid in school for once, all because of you.

You know what you have to do, Mom.

THE PRINCIPAL'S BEST FRIEND

Matt, comic

I don't know where that came from. I never saw it before. Honest! Someone must have written on my hand at lunch. I fell asleep. At the lunch table.

(Looking around the room.) Who did this to me? Do you think it's funny? Putting the answers to today's test on my hand? That is so lame. And very dishonest. Mrs. Stinkhauser and I are very disappointed in you!

Did I say — No, no! I didn't say Stinkhauser. I said Simhauser. Your name. I said your name. Mrs. Simhauser. And, and, and —

Look, I've got to go. I think the principal's missing me. I haven't been to his office yet this week and he gets lonely. So . . .

(Backing away.) I'll be going now, Mrs. Stinkhauser.

SEX ED

Jon, comic

No! It doesn't work like that! It can't! That's disgusting! And I, for one, don't look like one of those diagrams.

Is this all a joke? I just cannot believe anyone would do any of this stuff. No way.

My parents did that? No *way!* Now you're really making me sick. I was made in a test tube or something. None of this stuff went on. I hatched. I'm sure of it.

Is it possible, Mr. Winters, that you bought the wrong book? I mean, I saw a commercial yesterday that said, "If you see this blue line, you're pregnant." I saw that blue line, but since I'm a boy, I know that's not possible. I can't be pregnant.

I'm just saying that I think there's a lot of confusion on this stuff and it's possible you're wrong about all this.

INSTRUMENTAL

Russ, seriocomic

Couldn't I try drums? Please? I'd practice all the time. I'd be
the best drummer you ever had in the school band. I swear!
(Beat.) I know I'm not supposed to swear, but how can I show
you I'm serious?

Well, if you already have a drummer, how about saxophone?
I bet I could wail on a saxophone. Well, what then? *(Beat.)* Are
you serious? No, really. The triangle? That's not even an instrument. OK, maybe it is but . . . It's — It's not very cool, the
triangle. You just sit around a wait to play one dinky little
note — ding! It's sad. It's a sad instrument. I can't do it.

Hey — how about cymbals? At least they make some serious noise. How about it? I can't wait to practice. I'm gonna jam!

NO H$_2$O

Ben, seriocomic

No. I don't want to. I'm watching TV now. Why should I? It's a waste of time. And I want to see the end of this show.

Showering is totally overrated, Mom. I'm not dirty. *(Beat.)* I do not smell! Maybe *you* smell, Mom!

OK, sorry! But I really want to see this, Mom. Can't you see I'm busy? *(Beat.)* Will you quit nagging me already? Honestly, Mom, I don't get it. Do you *see* any dirt? I am a clean guy. I changed my shirt when I got home from school and everything.

Oh, please. PLEASE don't talk to me about hormones and growing up, Mom! It's gross. Let's just stop talking about it, OK?

Don't call me a "little man"! You can't make me do this. You're not going to win this one, Mom. I'm not going to crack. Ever.

LARGE AND IN CHARGE

Greg, seriocomic

This room looks fantastic. It's exactly how I want it. I know where my blue shirt is. It's over there in the corner. And my hockey stick is under there. I know where everything is. I'm in control.

Cleaning it would ruin everything. This is a work of art. Everything *does* have a place. Drawers are for losers. My *jeans* are over there. I told you. I have a *system*. Don't mess with it. Just because you can't understand it —

I'm not talking back. I'm explaining. *(Beat.)* Sure. Finc. You can take all my furniture away. Like I said, I don't need it. Drawers are for losers.

No! You can't take my CD player away, too! That's not furniture! That's cheating. You play dirty, Mom.

OK! OK! I'll clean it!

FAMILY VACATION TO HELL

Dermot, comic

She started it! I'm just sitting here. Minding my own business. Did you know she has the sharpest elbows in the entire universe? It's true. It's scientifically proven. By the way, this is a cruel and unusual psychological experiment, Mom and Dad. It's like a clown car in here. Like a bad joke. "How many family members can you fit in one car?" "How long will they last before someone gets killed?"

OK. I guess that's not funny. The killing part. But geez! We're all cramped back here and if you move around or you get sick of hearing "easy listening 101" on the radio or you make a *normal* comment you get yelled at around here. It's not fair. And I'm *not* sitting next to *her* any more. At the next rest stop, we part ways. You sit on *that* side of the car. I've had it. You keep your pointy elbows away from me, witchy.

OH, BROTHER, MY SISTER

Dylan, seriocomic

Don't stand too close to me. Don't look at me! Pretend you're by yourself. I just don't want anyone to think I'm with you.

I don't know which Hello Kitty pencil is better! It's just some stupid cat without a mouth. Come to think of it, that's really creepy. Besides, I don't like pink or purple.

Are you done yet? I can't believe Mom and Dad made me hang out with you! Just because we're related . . . Isn't that their job, anyway?

Listen, do you even have any money? *(Beat.)* No? Then why are you taking a half hour to decide which pencil is better when you can't even buy one? Come on. Let's get out of here.

Aw, OK. I'll hold your hand. Let's just go already.

WAR STORY

Mike, dramatic

My dad is somewhere overseas. In the marines. I don't know where. He's not allowed to tell us. I miss him. We used to have a lot of fun. We write him letters now. Sometimes we even get some back. But it takes a long time.

I wish he was back here. I wish I knew how long he'd be away. Now it's just me and Mom and David. I'm the man of the house. I've never thrown out the garbage so much in my life.

I know Mom is worried, but she pretends not to be. David doesn't know what's going on. He still asks for Dad sometimes. He's little. I wish I knew what to do to help. I'd throw out the garbage every day for the rest of time if that would help.

I heard Mom crying last night. I guess I'm not a very good man of the house. I'll have to try harder. Until Dad comes home.

BEHIND THE SCENES

Marcus, seriocomic

Does everyone have to audition? Because I'd rather not. I'm OK with being a tree or a rock. Or helping out with lights or something.

Please, could we just skip all this? I'll level with you. I can't sing. When it's someone's birthday in my family, they ask me to hold the cake. When I was little, I didn't know I stunk, and in church people used to turn and stare at me. I thought it was because I was cute! Now I know. And I don't want anyone staring at me ever again.

I'm doing a public service. My sister told me my singing sounds like a dying turkey. I've never heard a turkey dying (which I'm pretty happy about), but I'm pretty sure that wasn't a compliment. She's not a very nice girl, my sister. She's not about to give me a compliment, if you catch my drift.

So, how about I paint the set? Is it a deal?

DON'T LOOK DOWN

Bryan, comic

For my science project, I studied —

Pssst. Mr. Jenson. Ipzay your lyflay! XYZipit. *(Beat.)* No, no! I'm not goofing around! I mean, do you understand Pig Latin? *(Beat.)* No, no, my project isn't in Pig Latin. It's just that — It's just that —

Fine! I'll get on with my project.

For my science project, I studied electricity and made my own little motor using batteries. When you touch the wires together, they cause the wheel to turn. And, in conclusion, your fly is down, Mr. Jenson.

(Beat.) I'm in trouble? That's the last time I try to help you. Next time I'll just let everyone laugh at you behind your back. Itebay eemay!

ARCH ENEMY

Neal, seriocomic

Uh, uh, Miss. Grant? Um, um — Excuse me? Mrs. Grant? *(Beat.)* Sorry, I know I'm not supposed to interrupt you, but — Sorry, but — please — I'm sorry but I just *have* to interrupt, please, Miss —

MISS GRANT, YOU ARE STANDING ON MY FOOT!

Those are some pointy shoes you have on. I'm sorry, Miss Grant, I'm sorry, but I just had to interrupt you. I couldn't take it anymore! Forgive me for saying so, but you really ought to give a guy a break sometimes. You never know when it might be important. Sometimes a kid like me might have something very important to say.

It's OK, Miss Grant. I understand. Rules and all that.

Miss Grant, I know I'm interrupting again, but — Maybe can I go to the nurse?

CARBONATED CHAMP

Max, comic

I can do better than that. Listen to this: *(Belches.)* Now that is a burp.

And the champion for the fifth afternoon in a row is . . . Max! And the crowd goes crazy. Calm down, everyone. I think I'll give a speech for my fans:

As the world's best belcher, I have to thank, first of all, Coca-Cola for making such a wonderfully fizzy drink. Second, and not least, I have to thank my mother. I remember when I was a kid, my mother pulled the car over to the side of the highway because she thought she heard sirens behind her. Like an ambulance. That was the beginning of my career as a human noisemaker. For, you see, there was no ambulance. It was only me. This early success cemented my desire to work on my noise-making skills, making me the man, the champion, you see today.

Thank you; thank you. Come back tomorrow and see me defend my record once again with some of the top belching athletes from the sixth grade at Montclair Junior High.

ONE BAD DAY

Sean, seriocomic

What? A test? She never told us we'd have a test! I'm sure of it! *(Beat.)* No, she didn't! What is it on? *(Beat.)* I was totally paying attention yesterday, and I didn't hear anything about a test! Now I'm going to fail. This is just perfect.

(Beat.) What? Hey! I didn't — It wasn't me! It was Kenny. I wouldn't do that. In fact, I never do that. So stop looking at me! Geez, it smells awful. Don't say "who smelt it, dealt it" because you smell it, too. It's atomic. Get me out of here! Seriously, that's nasty, Kenny.

(Running to the other end of the room.) So tell me what I need to know for this test and make it loud because I am not getting anywhere near you!

FRIDAY'S LUNCH

Malcolm, seriocomic

I don't feel great. I don't know what's wrong. I just feel a little off. Phew. It'll pass. *(Beat.)* Yeah. I'm OK.

No, I don't have anything to share with the class. I just said my stomach hurts. *(Beat.)* No, I don't have to go to the nurse. *(Beat.)* Yes, I'll be quiet then.

Phew. What was in that lunch? I knew I shouldn't have eaten the fish sticks. I'm not gonna barf on you. Take it easy, bro.

Sorry. Sorry. I'll keep it quiet. I promise.

God. Oh. Phew. I don't feel so good.

Mrs. Sullen? Mrs. Sullen? I think I do have to —
Uh-oh! Here come the fish sticks!

FOILED AGAIN

Mark, comic

(Staring.) I'm squeezing your brain. With my mind I will stop the blood flow to your other organs. *(Concentrating.)* Your tongue will hang out of your head. You will drool like a baby. Your eyes will roll into the back of your head. Your head will fall back behind you. You're going to fall to the ground and quiver like the big, dumb moron you are. And your spleen will come out of your nose. *(Concentrating!)* Or, you will kiss Liz Perry, the girl of my dreams, and eat my lunch, chewing with your mouth open. Someday, Mike Barowsky, someday, I will master mind control! And you'll be so dead.

Until next time.

THE PLAYER

Derek, seriocomic

I'm sorry.
I am.
I shouldn't have said it.
It was thoughtless.
It was stupid?
I'm sorry forever?
Listen, I don't know why I did it.
I don't.
I was just trying to . . . I don't know.
I didn't think you'd want other people talking about us.
I guess I could have said it differently.
I could have said, "No, we're not together."
Would that have been OK?
Would that make you happy?
Clearly calling you, what I called you, wasn't necessary.
I could have just said it without calling you . . . what I
called you.
So, how about I just don't say it anymore.
And . . . I'll tell them I didn't mean it.
That I think you're nice.
And pretty.
And . . . that we're . . . that I like you.
How about that?
Huh?
Can we make out now?

GOLF COURSE OF ACTION

Colin, seriocomic

I'm totally nuts about you. I am. I know we just met, but sometimes you just know.

I do track. I'm a runner. It's cool. It's good for guys with
slim physiques, like me. I'm built for speed.

Hey, Paul. Wussup, man? *(Pause.)*

You two used to go out, didn't you? You and Paul? It must
be kind of awkward being in the same room and all.

Want to go to the golf course? It's so loud here. We could
get to know each other. Talk. Whatever.

You will? Yeah? You sure? 'Cause I don't want to twist your
arm or anything.

(Shocked.) OK. OK. We'll go to the golf course. *(Standing
still.)* We'll go now. *(Standing still.)* OK. Cool.

DREAM ON

Austin, comic

What did I do? Be honest. I can take it — I just don't know why, why, *why* she left me! We were perfect together. Just hanging out was fun. I remember how we laughed: "ha, ha, ha." I'll never forget that laugh. We liked all the same things — pizza, soda, movies, lunch, her hair — everything! Tom, she liked baseball. Baseball! How am I going to find another girl who likes baseball? Girls don't like baseball!

She thought my drawings, the ones I've been working on my entire life pretty much, she thought they were cute. And I . . . I was *good* to her. I bought her earrings for her birthday, candy on Valentine's Day, a turtleneck for Hanukkah — What more can a man do? I gave her everything! I thought we'd go to the prom together and she'd ask me to dance with her and I'd say "no way" and she'd laugh "ha, ha, ha" and say "kiss me, you fool — "

Uh . . . I can't lie to you Tom. She'd say something like that. I'm sure of it.

If I had a motorcycle, do you think she'd come back to me? How about a scooter? I won't be able to drive for a few years yet.

THE NEED FOR SPEED

Fred, seriocomic

This is it. I've worked for this for my entire life up to now. Every quarter my grandparents gave me, every scrap of my allowance, every birthday check stuffed in a card. Look at it. Shiny, new, bright, made for speed.

I hate it.

I have no idea why I wanted it so badly.

I hate it, Harry! What am I going to do? I want my money back, but I can't. I used it. I rode all around town on this boring thing. It looked so fun when other people were on them! It looked like they moved fast. It looked easy.

It's loud. It's slow. And I feel like an idiot riding it. *I — just — feel — so — stupid!* How could I be so dumb? Why didn't you warn me? *(Quiet, calming down.)*

(Suddenly.) AAAAAAAAAAAAAAAAAAAAAAHHHHH-HHHHHHHHHHHHHHHH! I am so mad at myself! I am stupid! A stupid, stupid, stupid, stupid, stupid, stupid —

Sorry, Mom, we're just rehearsing for a play. It's called, uh, *Scooter Boy and His Really Terrific Motor Scooter*. We'll keep it down.

FOUL WEATHER FRIEND

Ty, seriocomic

Hi. I guess we're caught here for a while. I didn't bring an umbrella either. I've never seen it rain this hard. Have you? *(Beat.)* No, this is pretty intense. So . . .

What's your name? I think you're older than me. *(Beat.)* Eighth grade. Wow. How's that? Eighth grade. Is it hard?

How come you're here so late? *(Beat.)* Your mom works? Mine, too. I was just walking around the woods back there. I think people hunt back there. Yeah. So I wouldn't suggest going back there. It could be dangerous. *(Beat.)* Yeah. No. I'm not planning to go back there again. I don't want to get shot or anything.

You think I'm cute? No one in my class thinks I'm cute. Oh, you mean little-kid cute. Thanks. Thanks a lot. My grandma thinks I'm cute, too. It's a gift.

I am a little funny. You like funny guys? Sooo, maybe in, like, ten years we could go out on a date or something. Maybe sooner. But I still think eighth graders are scary so it might take a while.

CAST OFF

Carter, seriocomic

(With two broken arms.) No, I don't need your help, Susie. Just put my book bag over my neck. *(Beat.)* Naw, really, you don't have to carry my books. I've worked this all out. If you just hook it over my head . . .

I've had some time to think about this in the hospital and perfect this system, Susie. *(Beat.)* Yeah, jumping off the top of the monkey bars was crazy. No, you don't have to sign my casts. I want my casts to be clean and white.

Yeah, some of the guys did sign it. *(Beat.)* OK, I'm going to have to be straight with you, Susie. Girls — Girls have germs that could infect my arm. The doctor told me that. *(Beat.)* Yeah, you can get an infection with broken arms. So, sorry to say this, Susie, but you're going to have to keep your distance.

See you in a few months.

BUSTING OUT

David, seriocomic

Hi, Suz. How was your summer? Hey, you look different! *(Beat.)* How? I don't know just . . . different. You're — taller. And — you just look really different.

Amber asked you to try out for cheerleading? I guess you're popular now, huh?

How am I supposed to know why she talked to you now? I'm not a genius.

(Beat.) I just said you looked different, that's all. Why are you pressuring me? *(Beat.)* I don't know *how*. I was just making a comment. Don't make a federal case out of it. Don't analyze it. Just — whatever. You look different. OK?

No! I did not notice that — that you — that you're all bigger . . . in some areas — *God!* You are so self-obsessed. Can't you women think about anything but your bodies? Give me a break!

FIRST DATE

Noah, seriocomic

So . . . That movie was interesting, right? I liked the part where the guy was walking. And he was talking to that other guy.

Hey, did you . . . I mean, what exactly . . . Did you get that movie? The commercials looked good. And there was that one funny part —

Yeah. That was the *only* funny part, wasn't it? And it was, like, six years long! How old am I now? Do I need a shave? Ha, ha.

The pizza's good though.

So . . . Did you see that movie about the robots taking over the earth and they can turn into monster-sized squirrels and they stomp all over buildings and there's this computer dude who has to save everybody but then he gets electrocuted and his assistant, a girl, has a find some computer file to erase the memory of the robots and this one guy gets stomped on and his eyes pop out —

No? Oh. It was good.

Hey, this pizza looks like the guy after he gets crushed! Ha, ha.

Sorry.

OUT OF THE OUTFIELD

Rob, comic

Guys, I'm really sorry. There was this bee in my eye. Right in my eye! And I couldn't see the ball. I thought it would sting me in the eye! You can imagine. I could be blind now. But I smacked that bee. I think I killed it. I'm OK now.

Is anybody listening? Guys, really, I'm sorry I let you down. It was just that bee —

I wasn't daydreaming! I was paying attention! Ready to go! Ready for action! And then that bee —

I won't shut up! You gotta understand I was in *danger*. I —

PLUS, no one ever actually hits the ball into the outfield! That's why I'm *in* the outfield, stupidheads! Everyone knows the outfield never has to do anything.

Stupid jerks.

RUNNING ON EMPTY

Josh, comic

(Jogging.) We've been doing these laps for hours now, I think. I know we have to be in shape to win games, but this is *(Gasping for breath.)* killing me. I'm tired. I want to take a nap. Could we at least mix it up and do other drills? It's all this back and forth, back and forth . . .

Sam, what happens when you're having a heart attack? Because I think I might be having one now. My chest hurts. My legs have gone numb. I'm cramping. I can't go on. I can't —

Call 911! I'm at death's door.

(Grabbing chest.) Can't go on — Heart valves blocked — Sam, sue McDonald's and tell my mother I love her —

Goodb — *(Collapsing.)*

SMOOTH OPERATOR

Javier, comic

Hello. You look *good*. I like the boots that you wear. *(Beat.)* You like my voice? My accent? My English is not good? *(Beat.)* Oh, it is? I am glad.

You are the first person to talk to me. I asked for New York, and I got New Jersey for school. Are they very different? *(Beat.)* I thought so. I thought "BIG CITY!" This is a city, Trenton, but it is a cruel city. Not the "get off my car, you stupid person!" cruel as the Big Apple is, but the "what are you looking at white boy" kind of city. Where I come from, being white is OK. Being black is OK. Whatever is OK. And why is it bad to look at people?

How about we get together over the weekend and you take me to Hollywood and Texas? You have a car? *(Beat.)* Texas is to see the cowboys, of course. Hollywood is to see the stars. You didn't know that? *(Beat.)* No cowboys?? Please, don't kid me I have seen the movies with Clint Eastwood. We will go see the cowpokes and then kiss. Pick me up at noon by the abandoned church.

BURNED

Steve, comic

Man, you have got to get out of the sun now! I'm not messing with you — you're in bad shape. You're a burner, not a tanner. Didn't you bring any lotion? *(Beat.)* You know, suntan lotion. Dude, how have you survived summer this long? You look like a lobster. Get in the shade.

Get me a Coke from the snack bar. And some cheese fries.

Hello, hello, ladies! I'm Mike. *(Beat.)* Him? He's Lobster Joe. Ha! Get it! Since he's so red. Like my savage tan? I've been working on it all summer.

You could rub some lotion on me.

Yeah, he's all red and he needs it, but —

I'll be at the snack bar if you need me.

THE POET

Brad, comic

Um, thanks for this, uh, award. It's great. The teachers asked me to read my award-winning poem. So, OK. Here we go. Don't get too excited and start screaming or give me a standing ovation or anything. OK. Here goes.

But first, let me say that we all did this assignment. It was assigned in English class.

Um, I got the idea for this poem from a TV show. Uh, it was a cop show. And there was violence. You know, the subject of our assignment. That we all did. I bet a lot of you wrote some really great poetry.

OK. Um, I'm supposed to get on with this. So I'll read my poem now.

Did I mention I won fifty dollars? That's more money than I've ever had.

OK! OK! My poem.

I wished for a time of rainbows

The bright daffodil —

Oh, the bell! Too bad. Back to class.

PAYBACK

Tony, seriocomic

Well, well, well. The day has come that I've been waiting for. Lookee here. I'm taller than you, Sara. Big sister, you're littler now.

Hmmmm. This is going to be interesting. I remember all those times you bossed me around. Told me I had to do what you said because you're bigger than me. You're not bigger any more. Look at you. You're so adorable. The little munchkin is trying to yell at me. It's like a little yapping puppy.

I remember the time you told me to go get the mail in my teeth from the mailbox. And the time you had me crawl on the floor so I could have a cookie when you were baby-sitting.

Bet you're sorry now. Don't worry; I won't take revenge. I'm above that. But things better change around here. You're going to start showing me some respect. Starting now. I think YOU should do the dishes tonight after dinner.

What? What's that? I can't hear you. You're going to have to speak up. I can't hear you from up here.

OBJECT OF DESIRE

Adam, comic

I just read in the paper, again, that this guy our age had a baby with his *teacher*. Again! It seems to be happening all the time. And the thing about it is — I think Miss Hutchinson — I think she has a thing for me! *(Beat.)* I am not joking! Think about it. She calls on me all the time in class, she tells me my answers are *very* good, she read my essay in class last week. She's got it for me — *bad. (Beat.)* Yeah. It is true. *(Beat.)* You see it, too? Well, what do I do? *(Beat.)* I couldn't do any of that with Miss Hutchinson. I could never kiss her even. I mean, she's — old, like thirty or something! And, but, I can't turn her down. She's my teacher! She'd fail me or something! What would I say? "Gee, thanks, Miss Hutchinson, I'm very flattered, but I've got this girlfriend in Mrs. Merrill's class (which everyone knows I don't) and we're very serious." I'm *thirteen*! I'm not ready for commitment and all that! This is HUGE, Matt, HUGE! What am I going to do?

DEATH BRING NOT CROWDS

Tim, dramatic

(*Looking in a coffin.*) Death. The final frontier. Man, this is creepy, bro. (*Sniffling.*) No, man, I am not crying. I dunno. I'm — (*Sneezing several times in a row, right over the coffin.*) Phew. I think it's these flowers. The white ones with the pink center. (*Beat.*) I don't know what they're called. What am I, a botanist? Oh, God, this is bad. I must be making us look good, serious grief, man. Seriously, it must be awful to be dead. No more chances. I mean, Uncle Larry didn't have kids or a wife. He just had us. Remember how he's play ball with us every Fourth of July? He was terrible. He just — made jokes and acted like a doofus his whole life. I don't want to die until I've *done* something. Something big. I don't know how most people can go on with their lives, being happy with just being a banker or something. That's no life at all. I don't want to have my best friends be some stupid kids.

I told you, man, I am *not* crying! Mom, tell him I have allergies!

FIELD TRIP

Harry, comic

Excuse me? Have you seen a large group of eleven year olds around here? *(Beat.)* No? Are you sure? There are a lot of them. Maybe you might mistake then for twelve year olds — seen any twelve year olds? *(Beat.)* No? OK. Thanks.

Hey, wasn't there a yellow school bus out here? *(Beat.)* Yeah! That's the one. Franklin School. Right. *(Beat.)* What!??! They left a half hour ago? But — but I'm here! I was supposed to be on that bus!

What am I going to do now? Is there anywhere to sleep here? Do you maybe have any jobs available? I would be an excellent tour guide. I could work in the mummy room with all the Egyptian stuff. That hook that pulled people's brains out is off the hook. Ha — that's pretty funny. I could tell a few jokes like: "Your mummy's so old she's preserved in a pyramid." That's good stuff. Don't steal it!

Oh, they're back! Hey, Mr. Harmon! Sorry I missed the bus. But never mind. I'm fine. I'm gonna stay here a while. *(Beat.)* Do I *have* to go back? Aw, OK.

Well, I guess I won't be staying. Let's "preserve" this time together in our memory. Get it! Preserve — like mummies! I'm on fire.

PAVAROTTI-TO-BE

Kevin, comic

(Singing in an opera singer–type voice.)
   Happy birthday to you,
   Happy birthday to you,
   Happy birthday —
What? How come everybody stopped singing? What's so funny? The candles are going to burn out.

   (Beat.) Me? What's so funny about me? *(Beat.)* The way I sing? I sing really well. My teacher says I'm the best singer in school. Just because I sing properly and support my sound — *(Beat.)* You're just jealous. You should be honored that I'd sing for you. I'm going to sing in Carnegie Hall some day.

   So let's hurry up while the candles are still burning. Besides, if I'm going to be an opera singer, I'd better get my weight up. I want to get as much of that cake in me as possible.

DOUBLE O NOTHING

James Bond, comic

Well, hello. Bond, here, James Bond. *(Beat.)* Yes, well, my mum couldn't come to Parent's Day 'cause she's traveling in Italy and my Dad is with the headmaster? I think they went to university together, Miss? So, no one's here to talk to my teachers but me. So, if you want to tell me about my academic performance, I'll be glad to pass on the information. *(Beat.)* No, I've done this before. It's on the up-and-up. I will tell them, Miss. I'm very trustworthy.

Yeah, well, I do keep to myself a bit. I like to watch other people. You see lots of things. For example, I know who blew the curve on your last test by cheating. *(Beat.)* I could tell you, Miss, but I don't think that's wise. *(Beat.)* Because I need to protect myself? And there is some benefit to having information people want to know? *(Beat.)* No, not blackmail, exactly. But if I should find myself in a bad situation, I can call on those individuals to help me out. It's diplomacy, Miss. *(Beat.)* No, I don't think I'll go into politics, with all due respect. I'm thinking I'll be a librarian. Or an English teacher. *(Leans in slowly.)* Like you, Miss.

FRENCH SMALL FRY

Napoleon, comic

I'm the boss of you and I'm the boss of you and I'm the boss of you and —

Don't interrupt!

I'm the boss of *you*. You, too.

Never call me shrimp. I am the boss of you! Did you forget? There will be desserts and chairs named after me! Napoleon! Leader! Ruler! King! Emperor! Where are you going? *(Beat.)* Russia? I'm coming too! Wait for me! I love cold weather! Hold on, guys! I'm coming with you.

Don't leave me here. I'm scared of the dark . . .

I RULE

Burger King, comic

I am your leader! Bow down! I am the Burger King. Let there be grease! Let them have apple pie with no apples in it and eat it too! Peasants, slaves, surfs, get me a Coke so large I can put my feet in it. Didn't you hear me? Do it now before I condemn you to garbage duty and the tyranny of the deep fryer.

You can't overthrow me. My name is on the sign.

There will be no democracy. You will toil forever under me.

I have a proclamation! "The Burger King makes no claim that there will be actual meat in the burgers, nor does he claim there will be no meat in the veggie burgers!" The king has spoken! Have a nice day!

THE SMARTASS OF STRATFORD

Will Shakespeare, comic

Milksop! Codpiece! If you come near me again, I'll festoon your pate with a cacophony of blows! Which will improve your looks, you son of a dog-faced strumpet!

What? What are you staring at? Never heard someone create language before? Is my massive intellect making you feel miniscule? Laugh if you will; if I be Will I do not mind.

No, calling me Shakesqueer is not creating language, you carbuncled dolt. Why am I cursed with such putrescence all about me? Woe is me, for all the world is filled with mediocrity. But I refuse to let it get me down into the bowels of Hades. I shall overcome even the harshest of thrashings and the mightiest of Nelsons. You may have the advantage of brute force, but I have a cranium chock-full of imaginings. You laugh now, but I will come out on the apex in the finale, minion. You will beg, sloven — I was kidding! Kidding! *(Grabbing nose.)* No! Refrain from rearranging my noble beak!

Help! Help, good people of Stratford! *(Running away.)*

BAKING

Hades, comic

One day my dad tells me to go to my room. So I do, because he's basically the most powerful guy in the universe. Next thing I know, I'm here in this world of eternal darkness, just me and my two little devil dogs, the Hounds of Hell. Sounds like a great name for a rock group, don't it? Man, I could go for a Twinkie. I don't have those down here. There's no baking in hell.

I really dug this Persephone chick, but she's not into me because she says I'm scary. People are so judgmental. I just look Goth because I was brought up this way. When you're in the depths of Hades (I renamed this place for me — what the hell, if I have to live here forever it better to be named after me), you can't really keep up-to-date with trends. Someone actually told me that metal is dead. That people listen to guys singing really high and sometimes those same guys are wearing braids? What is going on up there? When I was alive *little girls* sang high and wore braids.

And all I hear all day from you babies is how unfair everything is for you. My *father* sent me to the *underworld*. FOREVER! What did your dad do? Tell you to finish your homework? Please. Get back to me when you have some real problems. And next time you come, bring chocolate-chip cookies.

NICKNAME CALLING

Ivan the Terrible, comic

Why do I have to be "the Terrible"? You get to be "the Great" and I get to be "the Terrible"? What did I do that's so terrible? And what did you do that's so great? I want to be "Ivan the Fantastic-Stupendous-Master-Meister" or "P. Diddy." One of those.

Why not? Why can't I pick my own name for the rest of history if you can? Hardly seems fair. You know, Catherine is calling herself "the Great," too. She is. Are you sure you didn't copy her? Maybe we should call her "Catherine the Stink" instead. That will drive her up a wall. Louis-Phillipe wants a nickname, too, but I told him his first name was too long and there was no way to add to it.

Hey, want to pillage tomorrow? Or take over another country? Asia is *huge* and up for grabs. *(Beat.)* So what if it's mostly ice? *(Beat.)* Persia? That's a rug, a cat — who cares about Persia? Whatever. You can go if you want, I'm going to stay here and have a snow cone in Siberia.

YOUNGER FRANKENSTEIN

Victor Frankenstein, comic

Here. I can fix that. Oh, sorry. I broke it. I can fix it! Honest. The other day I brought a frog back to life with my dad's jumper cables — *(Beat.)* No, I did! I'm going to figure out how to bring people back to life. *(Beat.)* I am! *(Beat.)* How? I don't know yet. Maybe I'll get some dead people from the graveyard — *(Beat.)* Well, if they died 'cause their heart didn't work I'll get another heart. *(Beat.)* So? If they died 'cause their brain didn't work, I'll get another brain. *(Beat.)* Don't you get it? If they died 'cause they don't have legs, I'll get other legs. *(Beat.)* It doesn't matter if I find ones the same size. They'll be so happy they're alive again; it won't matter. I'll be famous. *(Beat.)* Shut up. When you die, I'm going to give you old-lady legs, and I won't need to replace your brain 'cause you don't have one.

TRENCHCOAT JUNIOR HIGH

Chandler, comic

Psst. Come over here. The lions growl at night. *(Beat.)* I said, the lions growl at night. *(Beat.)* Don't mess with me. We both know why we're here. The eagle flies over the nest.

Sooooo . . .

Don't you have something to tell me? *(Beat.)* "Nice night"? What does that mean? The bureau didn't tell me about this. Nice night? Are you *sure* that's what you want to say to me? Do you want to give you a little time to remember what to say?

Where are you going? Our "conversation" is not over! *(Yelling.) The pigeon sits on the statue! The rhino charges the jeep!* Oh, I am gonna be in big trouble. I'll never get onto the next stage in spy school! Did I say spy? No, no. I meant, uh, bag boy. Bag-boy school. That's where I'm going. They teach it at the Superfresh on Thursday evenings.

I gotta go now.

Female or Male
Monologues

FLIGHT

Alex, comic

This is cool. We're on the runway. About to take off. Into blue skies.

Where is the barf bag? *(Beat.)* No, I'm not worried. I'm fine. I'm fine. I was worried about YOU, Dad. You look a little off.

What's that? What's going on? *(Beat.)* Oh. Moving into position before we take off. Take off. We're going to take off. Up, up, and away! Very exciting. Oh, yes. This is grrreat.

So, where is that card explaining what to do in case of emergency? Someone has to know. Just in case. And the exit is — where? How are we supposed to get out with all these people in our way?

Yeah. I'm calm. Are you sure you're OK, Dad? 'Cause if you're nervous —

OK. OK. Thanks, Dad. I really need to hear that. It's gonna be OK.

(Beat.) If we land on water, can I use you as a floatation device, Dad?

ROCK ON

CJ, comic

WHAT? *(Beat.)* OH, YEAH, IT WAS GREAT! BEST CON-CERT EVER! I WAS SO GLAD THEY PLAYED THAT SONG! *(Beat.)* YOU KNOW, THAT SONG THAT'S OFF THEIR NEW CD? THAT SONG? *(Beat.)* YEAH! THAT'S THE ONE.

DID YOU BUY A T-SHIRT? *(Beat.)* WHAT? *(Beat.)* WHAT? *(Beat.)* OH, YEAH, YOU'RE WEARING IT. DUH. WHAT? *(Beat.)* OH, I SAID "DUH." NEVER MIND!

I CAN'T HEAR ANYTHING! CAN YOU? *(Beat.)* I SAID, "CAN YOU?" HEAR ANYTHING? *(Beat.)* NEVER MIND! MY HEAD IS RINGING LIKE QUASIMODO'S! IN THE BELL TOWER? LIKE MY SISTER'S PHONE ON SATURDAY NIGHT! I SAID — *(Beat.)* NEVER MIND.

MAN, THAT WAS ONE GREAT CONCERT! I DON'T THINK I'LL HEAR ANYTHING MY PARENTS SAY FOR A MONTH!

GIFTED AND TALENTED

Jack/Jackie, seriocomic

Make a picture. On this paper. It's graph paper. On purpose? So . . . I'm supposed to make square things? Can I see what someone else did?

OK, OK. I'll draw a car. With square wheels. No. No. It's just not possible to be creative with squares. So I guess instead of going into the gifted and talented program, you'll put me into the slow class now.

Hey, I know what this is about. Seeing if I can think outside of the box! Think outside the lines!

It's not about that. I'm really supposed to make square pictures. I could make a house. A house. This is boring. Can we just call the whole thing off? How can you *judge* a person's creativity anyway? What's the formula? How many square things a person can draw?

Why is the measure of being smart always doing what the teacher thinks you *should* be doing? Did you ever think that maybe I could maybe be even smarter than you, so I wouldn't think what you were thinking, I'd be thinking something even better?

OK, fine. I'll draw the car with square wheels. Are you happy now?

ESSAY AGONY

Geri/Gerry, seriocomic

What I Did This Summer by Me. This summer, I went to —
This summer, I —
This summer, I did nothing. I ate cookies in front of the TV.
I played video games. I read some books. I made hot dogs for
me and my brother. I watched a lot of cartoons. I went to Con-
necticut to see my grandparents. That's it.

I'm sorry. We just don't go anywhere. My mom and dad
work during the day. And we can't go on big vacations. It's kind
of boring. But I wrote a really good story about what I wish I
did this summer. It has everything — action, adventure, sun-
tans — I save the world *and* I learn to surf.

I really hate this assignment. When I go to college, will I
still have to do this assignment? If I do, I am definitely going
to be a truck driver instead. It's lame.

MAKING IT COUNT

Chris, comic

How do you know? Just because I count all the time doesn't mean I'm crazy. So what that I know it takes sixty-two seconds from when you can first see the subway on Eighty-sixth Street to when it pulls into the station and the elevator in my building takes six seconds between floors and five seconds for the doors to open and close? What's so abnormal about that? It's *curiosity*. Shouldn't you be rewarding me for that?

No. No, thanks. I couldn't. I can't. I don't shake anyone's hand. So see, no offense, it's just not gonna happen. I don't know where you've been. What's in my backpack?

Well, if you must know it's filled with stuff. Purell — no, I still won't shake your hand — wet-naps, antibacterial cleanser, tissues, Tupperware —

Well, that's personal. Fine! I do not want to touch anything in a public bathroom. That's what the Tupperware is for. I throw it out right away. Afterwards. It's not gross because it's not as if I keep it! I rarely use the bathroom anyway except at home. It's just for emergencies. *And do you mind not tapping your pen on your desk?* You've done that sixty-two times already and it's beginning to annoy me! And I really don't like the number sixty-two, and I try to avoid it if I can.

FOREVER ME

Jordan, comic

I *really* want it. Just because I'm young doesn't mean that I can't make good decisions. You can't know that I won't be able to make a life-long decision. You're not psychic.

I'm so good. I get good grades. I *deserve* this. I promise it won't be a battleship. Or snakes. Or my [girlfriend/boyfriend's] name; I'm not so dumb to think we'll be together forever — I'm only [thirteen]. I don't know what it'll be. Or where it'll be. But it won't be somewhere obvious. Or somewhere gross. Or anywhere I'll get really fat.

I just love the idea that you can do something permanent. Something that will remind me of where I was and who I was, years and years from now. *(Beat.)* Don't interrupt — please. I've thought very, very hard about this. Tattoos have been used throughout the ages to celebrate cultures, to show status, as works of art! It is something ancient tribes did and still do — not just rebellious teenagers. You have to go through pain to create something beautiful. It's not easy. It's not something you do without careful consideration. I have taken that careful —

I told you not to interrupt! How can you say no? You didn't even let me finish! Now maybe I will get a battleship. Then you'll be sorry!

WAITING

Jaime, comic

Aaaaah! Hurry up, bus! I am so sick of waiting! It's fr-rrrreeeezing. When do we give up and go home? Maybe it's a snow day and no one told us! Maybe the bus is never coming. I'm going to count to ten and if the bus doesn't come, I'm going home.

One. Two. Three. Four. Five. Six. Seven. Eight. Nine. Ten.

No bus! Let's beat it. I'm outta here. Come on, we can go. The bus is twenty minutes late and it's freezing! It's probably not safe to drive and it's way too cold to stand out here! *(Beat.)* Aaaaah! It's so cold! I don't care if I get in trouble. That's it. I'm counting to ten one more time. One *last* time. Then I am going home. And you should leave, too! *(Beat.)* Don't be such a goodie-goodie. It's twenty-two minutes late, Lisa. OK. I'm counting to ten.

One. Two. Three. Four. Five. Six. Seven. Eight. Nine. Nine and a half —

Let's go! I said ten! I said ten before it came! Oh, my life stinks.

REBEL

Cole, comic

This is cruel. We have to sit here selling baked goods and don't get to *have* any unless we pay for them. We made them! Or at least some people in our class made them.

Stephanie is such a Nazi. The bake-sale Nazi. She thinks just because she's president of our class she's actually in charge. She is just a figurehead. We are in [sixth] grade, for god's sake, she has no actual power. She's just class president because someone has to be class president and she's the Naziest one in the class so she has to be the best at everything.

Except she's in my math class and I am way smarter than her. I just don't want to be class president.

And *I want a doughnut!* You in with me? *(Beat.)* Yeah? On the count of three. One, two, three —

(Beat.) Oh, hi, Stephanie! Great to see you! Everything's cool out here.

. . . IN A BOTTLE

Gene/Jeanne, comic

What can I do for you? *(Beat.)* Not again! How did this rumor get started? I'm afraid there is no such thing as a genie in a bottle. *(Beat.)* Who am I? I'm a genius in a bottle, of course. Sooo, what can I do for you? Discuss the origins of the universe or prove (or disprove) the existence of God or explain the theory of relativity —

You want me to tell you why your life is a graveyard of buried hopes. OK. Let's see. We can approach this from several directions. Genes are the building blocks determining —

No? OK. Plato believed we all come into the world as a *tabula rasa* — a blank slate — and that it is our environment which shapes us, giving way to the modern notion that our problems derive from our upbringing —

No again? Feudal societies, like that of medieval England, based their civilizations on the notion that you are born into a certain role in life: serf, knight, king . . . It is only with the birth of democracy that we see people striving to live beyond the socioeconomic station they are born int —

You mentioned earlier you'd like to be rich. I think I can hack into a bank's computers. OK? Happy now? *(Beat.)* Sure, sure, I'm a genie, whatever.

HEAVEN

Mel, comic

Hi. I'm dead. It's actually not creepy. It's a little boring some-times. I don't know exactly where I am. At first I thought it was heaven because I get to eat all the fast food I want or I can chow down on only dessert, but now I'm not so sure. Someone told me cholesterol is still an issue here. You know, high blood pres-sure and all that. There's no money, though. I can just say, I want to ride a bike and — poof! — there's a bike. *(Beat.)* Sorry, Jimmy, that was just an example. I don't really want the bike.

Yeah. That's Jimmy. He's just the guy with the bikes and cars. Roger is the guy with the video games. I'll give you a tour later. *(Beat.)* You need the bathroom? *Tony!* He musta done something bad, I think. *Tony!* Don't tell him you stocked up on the chili, he'll get mad.

ABOVE IT ALL

Lex/Lexie, comic

Naw, I'm completely relaxed. How many times have you done this? *(Beat.)* Thousands? Yeah, I feel pretty safe. I'm not scared easily. Not phobic. I love adventure! And I've got an expert helping me out, right? I'm psyched! My friends call me Dare, 'cause I'll take on any dare. Ask me to do anything. *(Beat.)* Jump? OK, let's do it —

(Pause. Speaking louder.) Hold on! Wait a second. *(Starting to hyperventilate.)* That wind is really strong! Whoa. *(Pause.)* How many times have you done this? *(Beat.)* Five thousand? How many people have died? *(Beat.)* None? How many have been maimed? *(Beat.)* Injured? *(Beat.)* OK. Mind over matter. That's a good record. Except — the law of averages might say that you have to crash sometime! Maybe five thousand and one is not your lucky number! I'm not so sure anymore. Couldn't we just say we did this? I think I changed my —

(Falling.) WHOOOOOOOOOAAAAA!!!!

BIAS

Jo/Joe, dramatic

What are you looking at? Is it OK if I look at this? Am I permitted? I am a potential customer. And this is a store? And a free country? You don't think I can pay for this, but I can. Just because I'm not an adult doesn't mean that I can't pay for anything. I save my money. It's so unfair. That you just follow people like me around. It's ageism. Ever hear of that? I could sue you. *(Beat.)* Ha, ha, ha. You think it's funny. Because I'm a kid. You won't be laughing when you're in court. You don't even make so much money anyway. I bet I make pretty much what you make. Not so funny now, is it? A shop girl. You're so smug. Well, I [baby-sit/mow lawns] and I make good money. I can pay for whatever I want, so leave me alone and let me look at things without you hanging over me!

OK, I want this. Wait, do you get a commission? *(Beat.)* Hold on, I'm going to find another salesperson.

LISTEN UP

Nick/Niki, dramatic

Don't I have any say in all this? *(Beat.)* You always tell me what to do and you *never* listen to me. And why should I listen to you 'cause you just screw everything up. *(Beat.)* Well, you're getting *divorced*, aren't you? That is not a sign of being really good at everything, being the smartest people in the world, being *understanding* and *compassionate*?

Don't laugh at me! What did I say that was funny? You were too smiling. This is not cute. This is not me being your cute kid.

You don't know what's best for me because what's best for me is to have a family, a whole family, where no one fights and you sit down and have dinner together and you ask me how school was. And I say "fine" and I mean it, I don't just say it to shut you up.

When do I get to have some say in things? Don't say it. Don't say, "When you're an adult." That's bull. When I do something bad, you tell me I'm grown up now and have to take responsibility for my actions, blah, blah, blah, but when I want to make a decision, it's "you'll do what I tell you to do" and "because I said so." Well, maybe it's time I did start acting like an adult and I'm going to start by telling you two to act your age and stop this divorce thing.

Because I said so.

STREET SCENE 1

Daniel/Danielle, dramatic

What are you doing here? I know why I'm here — my parents don't much care if I get shot or anything. My mom told me to *walk* to school today. A kid was shot near here last week!

This whole thing — what's going on in the world is so messed up. The whole world hates us. Terrorists. I don't know. There must be something more than *our* perspective. If *every* other country thinks we're wrong, maybe there's something to that. Maybe we are big bullies. There might be something there. Why do we have to be the biggest and the strongest? Why are we always the ones fighting? How come other people get to make these decisions for *me* that affect my life? I just want to wake up someday and not be afraid I'm going to be bombed or shot or anything. I want to feel safe.

(Beat.) I know you think being the strongest and being aggressive will keep us safe — but what if you're wrong? I don't think people in Monaco or Chad are maybe fearing for their lives like this.

STREET SCENE 2

Rich/Rachel, dramatic

I think we just need to stand up to people. Not be intimidated. That's why I'm not backing down, staying at home . . .

Everyone who threatens us should be made into dust. A parking lot. If we let stuff go, we'll get bitten in the butt. We can't let that happen. I don't see why we have to explain it and ask permission either. Just go in there and get the job done! It's easy. Maybe not easy, but — no, it is. We have the power. Use it. Like if you're a teacher or a parent. You use your power. Whether you think you are or not. Everyone gets off on power, and what's wrong with that? When I'm a senior, I'm going to give freshmen a hard time. And when I have kids, I'm going to boss them around, and when I'm a boss, I'm going to get my assistant to do everything. Why not? Survival of the fittest. It's the way of life.

I just had the feeling like we ought to join hands and sing songs from *The Lion King*.

I'm kidding about the singing, but it is all about the circle of life.

(Beat.) You shouldn't worry. Everything's gonna be fine. You should trust people more.

THE AUTHOR

Kristen Dabrowski is an actress, writer, acting teacher, singer, and director. Kristen began her career in children's theater and musical theater; since then, her roles have run the gamut from Greek tragedy to contemporary comedies. She received her MFA in performance from The Oxford School of Drama in Oxford, England. Kristen has performed at several regional, Off Broadway, and international theaters such as McCarter Theater, Battersea Arts Centre, the John Houseman Theater, and Tricycle Theatre. The actor's life has taken her all over the United States and England. She is a member of the Actors Equity Association. Currently, she teaches acting, voice, and dialect classes in New York City. You can contact the author at monologue madness@yahoo.com.